Saving The
WHOLE
Child

Saving The WHOLE Child

A Grandmother's Personal Experiences
Living with Teen Grandsons

Ms. GG

SAVING THE WHOLE CHILD
A GRANDMOTHER'S PERSONAL EXPERIENCES
LIVING WITH TEEN GRANDSONS

iUniverse books may be ordered through booksellers or by contacting:

iUniverse
1663 Liberty Drive
Bloomington, IN 47403
www.iuniverse.com
1-800-Authors (1-800-288-4677)

Because of the dynamic nature of the Internet, any web addresses or links contained in this book may have changed since publication and may no longer be valid. The views expressed in this work are solely those of the author and do not necessarily reflect the views of the publisher, and the publisher hereby disclaims any responsibility for them.

Any people depicted in stock imagery provided by Thinkstock are models, and such images are being used for illustrative purposes only. Certain stock imagery © Thinkstock.

ISBN: 978-1-5320-3393-3 (sc)
ISBN: 978-1-5320-3392-6 (e)

Library of Congress Control Number: 2017915035

Print information available on the last page.

iUniverse rev. date: 10/04/2017

DEDICATION PAGE

To Families, Parents, and Caregivers

This Book is dedicated to you—We share a life filled with happiness, pain, many tears as well as the Joy we receive when we see positive change in our loved ones no matter how fleeting the moment.

You my dear readers and I share what I call the roller coaster ride of emotions, on a daily basis. Just know, every sacrifice if worth it.

Always remember to

STAY FOCUSED AND STAY STRONG

I EXTEND TO YOU A WORD OF ENCOURAGEMENT:

PERSEVERE

CONTENTS

PREFACE

"Our lives begin to end the day we become silent about things that matter." Dr. Martin Luther King

The traditional role for grandparents is for the grandchildren to visit, enjoy being spoiled, and then returned to their parents. Imagine my surprise when one day I asked myself, 'did these children move in and no one told me?' Sadly, I really wasn't expecting a call. Quickly, I found myself the Custodial Grandparent to two identical twin grandsons. This title was given to me by a Family Court Judge.

Becoming a caregiver for my grandsons who both have the diagnosis: Attention Deficient – ADHD, Oppositional Defiance, Emotional Disturbance, Autism Spectrum as well as several mood disorders was tough. I love my grandsons and I am dedicated to do everything necessary to see that they are well taken care of, but most importantly—they will feel loved.

There was no doubt in my mind that I would need to become an advocate for my grandsons. Blinded by the enormous task of parenting special needs children, I was overwhelmed. Equipped with a little information but many unanswered questions, I began my search to find the needed information for my boys. There had to be information out there but finding it proved to be a big fat headache.

On the positive side, I've learned from families and caregivers that we have similar situations and various diagnosis'. This means we are dealing with the same issues—securing the needed help to save our children. This was not only comforting but also encouraging because I didn't feel like I was alone in this battle. The decision was then made to share my experiences in a book form for several reasons.

First, through research I found that there are many resources available, but for some reason this information is difficult to acquire. Secondly, there are a vast number of situations or incidents that my grandsons encounter that leave me puzzled. Children's mental health issues are a daily part of our lives. There isn't a day that passes where an outburst at school, on the playground, or even at church that something happens.

As their guardian, it is then left on me to fix their multitude of problems that involve them. On numerous occasions, I have found myself in situations feeling helpless. Because I had no idea of the seriousness, nor had I accepted the fact that I needed help—I didn't know where to find the required information. Thirdly, I wasn't prepared for the impact that changed our family relationships. Seriously, I became concerned that without guidance the new aggressive, explosive behaviors that began to surface would destroy my family in ways I wasn't prepared for.

Certainly, there are skeptics who may ask, 'what makes me qualified to even speak on the subject about mental health and its accompanying issues.' It's simple, I am qualified because I am living this life. Participating in parent/caregiver training sessions which taught techniques and strategies used to assist special needs children qualifies me. Constantly I am communicating with the CSE, (Committee on Special Education), in my boys' school.

Parents must get control of the suspensions our special needs children face daily which are generally due to behavior. Regrettably so, I have found inexperienced faculty members who are not trained to work with our children who require a variety of methods to assist them in the classroom. It is impossible to send our children to school and assume all is well. Assuredly, I can confirm that in many instances that is not the case.

Initiating surprise visits not only regarding staff but also to see what my precious angels are doing have proven successful. Before long, I became a parent advocate at my boy's school, where I attended meetings with parents who were meeting with the committee on special education. Initially, I was there mainly for support, other times to nudge parents to ask questions of the team that I knew needed to be heard.

Eventually, I learned that most of the parents felt that they had to accept everything the committee presented. NO WAY. Happily, I would always interject that parent input was important. The result of the meeting must follow the IEP which is a legal document and must be adhered to. Parents must speak out, that is one thing I do not have a problem doing. Prepared with questions, I expect the discussion to continue until all issues are understood.

Currently, I am a former member of the Family Advisory Board, at the Day Treatment School my boy's attend. Also I am a retired music teacher that worked with elementary public-school students. Along with being the custodial guardian of my daughter's twin boys, I am an adoptive parent of four special needs siblings.

For eight years I served as director over the Youth Department within my church affiliation. From the State Department of Education and Children Services, I received recognition for my work with adoptive parents and children. Most importantly in my book is thirty-three years qualification assisting children and families. Assisting families to find the necessary resources needed to gain control of their lives and emotions, as well as the need to understand the challenges children and families face daily.

Advocacy for children and families with special needs, I feel is something every child needs from their parent. Being a big supporter of parent support groups, I search for them because they are an excellent learning tool. Support groups also give others the opportunity to meet families and share experiences. Calmness instantly covers me being around people who would rather not throw negativity into the universe. Only positive ideas and thoughts are shared for everyone present has to deal with serious issues. Sometimes, I have found that we just need to be able to laugh, embrace meeting new friends, take a little time to ourselves, and be happy. Normally, I am always worried, thinking, and searching for ways help my boys. But I realized that if I didn't take a moment for myself, it just made our journey more difficult.

Then the indication of an aha moment appeared to me, I have a story to tell. Spending a great deal of time on the technical aspect of my mental health journey, I felt that since it was interesting to me it would be interesting for others to read, "Saving the Whole Child." Slowly, I began to realize that how could I ask or really expect the therapists and other providers to actual listen to our problems when I hadn't used my voice effectively.

While initially I just wanted to share the experiences my boys and I have endured, but I've come to realize it is a much bigger problem that all families with special needs children face. The only thing that I know without a doubt is there must be a major change in this massive mental arena. Everyone has experiences and various situations they deal with. The experiences you will read in "Saving the Whole Child" are real, factual, and most importantly—they are mine. One of the most important things that I want to share, parents and caregivers, you are your child's best advocate.

CHAPTER ONE

Classroom Problems: Identifying Problem Behaviors And Developing a Course of Action

"Life is the ultimate teacher. Life always has a unique way of giving us what we can handle."

My grandsons were in the first grade when both of their teachers contacted me to discuss the behavior issues the boys were having in school. Now, the boys are identical twins and were exhibiting the same behaviors. Academics for both boys was never a problem but their inability to control themselves was a major concern.

My young men were constantly disturbing the other students, such as randomly running in and out of the classrooms, making loud noises, and just having a wonderful time. Every once in a while I would walk into the classroom for a surprise visit because I wanted to see for myself just what was happening. Imagine my surprise when I found the teacher in tears, almost ready to pass out from chasing one of my angels who had decided to play hide and seek.

It was explained to me that if the regular classroom teacher was not in the classroom, they would act out. Basically if there was a substitute teacher or teachers assistant in charge, their behavior was out of control. The slightest change in their routine became problematic.

They were in separate rooms yet the behavior was the same. They were constantly walking out of the classroom without permission. For some reason, they loved to roam the building, running, and just having a good old time. They enjoyed making the building their indoor playground complete with staff on the chase. Another fundamental problem, as if we didn't have enough, just a simple touch on the shoulder or a gentle touch on the hand, turned into a serious screaming match.

Any one of these scenarios would require that I be contacted to come and take one or both boy's home. This repeated action was a constant problem for me because I worked at a different school. Just packing up and leaving was impossible. Further problems arose when the boys had their own opinions about how they felt having to be removed from the classroom. They expressed how the other students felt or acted toward them.

Not to mention teachers and other adults would talk where the children could hear, this only made the situation worse. "Adversity is that hated friend sent to try us, who makes us stronger." We could only see the behavior, at this stage I didn't understand anything that was going on. Their feelings about the way they thought they were being treated especially worried me. The three of us were simply trying to exist during an imperfect situation.

There was so much I didn't know. Quickly I realized that I had to take a crash course in learning the system so that I could get the needed help for my boys. First, I must begin by saying it is important that you be in contact with your child's school administrators, social worker, and most important there must be ongoing dialog with the classroom teacher. This turned out to be not only a valuable resource but the combination of knowledge from these professionals is what guided my initial involvement into the world of children's mental health.

The school social worker could arrange to have the boys tested by a Board Certified Behavioral Development Pediatrician who provided Neurological assistance for school age children. I chose the social worker and one of the boy's teachers to be present when the results of the testing would be discussed. This teacher's son was diagnosed with Turret Syndrome. As this was unfamiliar territory for me, I knew that I needed to upstart my education by surrounding myself with professionals who could give me the correct advice needed. This was too important to make a mistake.

Being a parent of a child that was diagnosed with a mood disorder, this teacher became an invaluable resource to me. She knew what questions to ask and what procedures we should seek. Believe me the process was scary because you become aware of the fact that you don't know how to help your child.

The reason for the Neurodevelopment Evaluation was to learn what problems existed. The boys exhibited signs of impulsivity, anger, and aggression concerns. The other areas of difficulty were oppositional defiance, emotional disturbance, and difficulty reading their writing samples. Language functions (expressive language) was more problematic than receptive, visual processing as well as short term memory.

The results of the testing and recommendations that were given thankfully were clear and helpful.

- Medication was strongly recommended with instructions that it be closely monitored by their pediatrician.

- Counseling was necessary for Behavior Management Training.

- Sessions for in-school Occupational Therapy.

- At school, creating a unified approach with the teachers to create autonomy in learning by utilizing adaptations as well as accommodations within each classroom.

The main testing areas of concern was the boys Developmental History, Social History, Behavioral/Social Skills, Educational History, and Family Social History. I've included this information because I was overwhelmed with the enormous amount of technical information. Fortunately, I had teachers who assisted me in this journey and I want to share my experiences with other families.

The result of the testing was a diagnosis of ADHD Combined Type because of the inattention, impulsivity, and hyperactivity that was the cause of significant impairment. Interestingly enough, the boys are identical twins and they each had the same diagnosis. Having already discussed the boy's issues with their pediatrician, I included his questions along with mine at the meeting. Now that we know we have a problem, we must define the cause(s) and the most important question I had, 'how do we fix this?'

Since medication was deemed necessary, I needed the doctor to give me suggestions as to what medication to start with, dosage, and most importantly instructions on how to administer them. LABELS, LABELS, LABELS, get used to them. I was informed that to get the help needed, a label is required. Even if the label if not accurate, it will serve as the vehicle to perhaps find out what the actual problem was.

Again, this is something else to get used to because I have had numerous encounters like this. Currently I am still learning the various terminology and techniques that will hopefully bring about a change from the negative behavior to positive behavior. One thing I know for sure, this journey would not be an easy one.

We were at the pediatrician's office where I saw a flyer from one of our universities. It was an announcement about a research study for various medications which were being tested for various medications for children diagnosed with ADHD. Thankfully the boys were accepted and the real work began.

The young people met weekly in group sessions which were all research based. We spent a year learning about ADHD medications, anger management, strategies for improving concentration, task completion, and social skills. Each study was for six weeks. The highlight of the program for me was while the staff of Psychiatrists and Psychologists worked with the children, the adults, parents, guardians, and other care givers, had our own experts working with us.

This experience was not only important but helpful to me because I learned that I wasn't the only one living with children with serious issues. The eye opener for me was when fathers shared their issues which were like mine, and they had the same difficulties that I had. My thought process was men rule the home and everyone listens. Not so; but in this setting, we all shared our experiences, fears, and thoughts without any negative comments. No one was offended or insulted, if anything we felt at peace, even if it was only for an hour.

The first research study that we participated in was for the medication Strattera. It worked for about one day. It was like giving the boys a drink of water. Trying to find the right medication is a trial and error process. Now, coupled with medications both boys resisted taking meds. Every day I heard the same thing; "why do I have to take this", I don't like how I feel", I on the other hand loved it, because for a few moments there was peace and quiet. Soon I began finding pills everywhere, their bedroom dresser, kitchen drawers, behind the toilet, believe it or not even in the driveway, chair cushions, everywhere BUT their tummies.

This was a never-ending problem. The research study included counseling, in-school visits to the teacher explaining and answering questions, and of course the issues of medication. This was all overseen by the Psychologist, and of course monitored by their pediatrician as well. An important aspect of this training that I learned was that mental health programs and interventions are all based on scientifically sound research. The parents would be given a situation to discuss and come up with a way to handle the situation. We were never given a yes or no answer, but the response was always, research states.

Everything about these training sessions was not only helpful but finally I was able to receive some much needed information. Having a child on medication requires a treatment plan with constant evaluation to insure there are no negative side effects. Treating children with ADHD requires medical, educational, behavioral, as well as psychological testing. Research shows that most children with ADHD, medication is a valuable tool to improve the symptoms but it does not eliminate them.

ADHD is a comprehensive disorder that leads to different behaviors among children and adults. While it originally stood for Attention Deficit Hyperactivity Disorder, many doctors have chosen to redefine it slightly because it is more than just attention deficit. Sometimes ADHD is standalone situation, but usually there are additional disorders prevalent. A fact that I found interesting was, males are three times more likely to be diagnosed with ADHD than females. For my family, I chose the route of medication but there are other options, such as therapeutic or holistic treatments.

Another major source to find research programs, search the colleges and universities in your area, the Department of Psychology Psychiatry, and the Department of Social Work. Every county and state government has an office of children services. Please don't forget your politicians on every level.

CHAPTER TWO

Counseling
Feel, Believe, Change

"YOU CAN'T TREAT A PROBLEM WITHOUT A SOLUTION."

I am a firm believer that talking to a trained professional is not only crucial for families but I have learned the importance of doing so. Yes, it's been a slow and painful process but the process and experience continues to be necessary. I finally realized that I benefited from the family sessions as much as my boys did. Actually, for children with ADHD and other mental health issues, it is highly recommended as a part of the therapy plan. My family has been involved with learning behavioral techniques, behavior therapy, play therapy, therapeutic techniques, as well as behavior modification.

Counseling has been and still is a necessary tool in helping the boys to manage their behaviors as well as the negative thought processes which symptoms of ADHD. It is my opinion that these sessions of talking as I like to call them, enables us to talk freely to someone who will listen to us without fear of judgment, and the chance to get valuable feedback.

We need to deal with the unresolved issues that many of us have encountered in this journey of life, children and adolescents are not exempt from this. There are times that I feel my mind could use a "tune-up" every now and then. I like to think that every experience can be turned into a beneficial learning experience.

Now the challenging work begins in finding a therapist, but more importantly how to find the right therapist to work with your family. It's best to start with your pediatrician, the school social worker, and the school counselor. I found it helpful to check with your school districts committee on special education for information.

First, we need to understand the diverse types of mental health professionals as well as who does what. A therapist is trained in Psychotherapy as well as Mental Health Counseling, they do not administer medications of any kind. Secondly, there are Social Workers who provide guidance to help people cope with challenges in their lives which include psychological counseling and assistance which is usually in the form of various social services.

Next, the Psychiatrist which is a medical doctor who is trained in treating mental health issues and prescribes medication. Finally, the Psychologist who evaluates and studies behavior and mental processes with the focus being on behavioral treatment.

An important fact that I must share is that you must realize and accept that counseling is a part of the treatment plan for your child; because the entire family is affected. There are several things I want to share, I feel this is important because a therapist stopped and assessed my behavior. They analyzed how my behavior was hurting and not helping my boy's change their behavior.

1. My reactions to certain behaviors were negative triggers for the boys. My tone of voice, even the words I used needed to change.

2. I allowed the boys to see my frustrations which were negative as a result of their behaviors.

3. I had to be taught behavior management skills. Instead of shouting five or six times different threats—get up, the bus is here, clean up your room—these are just a few. The therapist helped me to realize that I needed to bring the number of commands down to no more than two times, with space in between the commands. I needed to become aware of my tone of voice, instead of yelling I had to learn to use my inside soft voice with NO FROWNS.

While I found the techniques difficult, and I will admit that I said, "why do I have to do these things, I'm not the one with the problem." Well, I soon learned just how much of the problem I was. I had to learn that my mindset had to change, yes it was difficult at first because I soon realized that I was out of my comfort zone. As I took a good look and thought about how my boys felt and what they were going through, I realized that I was a contributing factor to the problem.

I really disliked talking about my feelings because I felt vulnerable, which caused me to think if I feel this way how do these children feel? Yes, it was uncomfortable but the result of these methods brought about a positive change, which made life in our household easier. Thankfully, that change was brought on by counseling.

The following things are facts that I found important when looking for a therapist that will be a good fit for my family.

---You must get the feeling right away that this person if nonjudgmental, and is not quick to give an opinion.

---I learned that it was important that when I began my search that

I kept an open mind. Since I didn't want anyone judging my family I had to do the same.

---Credentials aren't everything. This doesn't give that person the ability to assess your family situation accurately, you must be aware of everything.

---I talked to people and collected names and phone numbers. I asked everyone for recommendations especially the boys pediatrician and school counselor.

---I was prepared for our first meeting with questions instead of coming unprepared. My gut feeling (some call it intuition) never leads me in the wrong direction.

---You have to make sure that the therapist that you finally chose to work with has the credentials and knowledge to correctly treat your child's diagnosis.

We have seen several therapists, almost too many to count. A few were disappointing at best, I mean totally no assistance was given, but we've also worked with several that were able to penetrate through to the boys, and I saw positive results. This is a trial and error process, we can only keep going. Stopping is not an option.

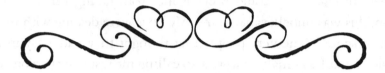

CHAPTER THREE

Special Education
Identifying Individuals Needs and Differences.

"SOMETIMES THE QUESTIONS ARE COMPLICATED,
AND THE ANSWERS ARE SIMPLE." Dr. Seuss

Considering the process for Special Education was my last option for help. There was relentless daily pressure from my grandson's teachers and staff regarding their behavior. By this time, I spoke to several mental health professionals whose only conclusion was: "Problem behaviors can be corrected, it just takes time." This was not what I needed or wanted to hear.

I discussed this latest statement with their pediatrician and he suggested I ask for a Functional Behavior Assessment. This assessment is to be given by the special education department in our school district. Having tried a series of trials with behavior therapy as well as medication that produced limited change in behavior, this seemed like my best option.

The Functional Behavior Assessment (FBA) is a part of the Special Education process which looks at specific student behaviors as well as determining what the child is trying to communicate through these behaviors. Special Education is really a unique tool that identifies the academic, physical, cognitive skills, as well as the social – emotional instructions. I saw first-hand that all these factors applied to my boys.

When I started my pursuit for finding out and learn just what the process entailed for getting my boys tested, I was pleasantly surprised to learn how extensive and inclusive this testing was. Sadly, two classroom teachers thought they could prevent me from taking this course of action; this was unbelievable to me. My boys were dealing with severe issues at school. The very people that thought they had a say in any decisions that I was making were also calling me just like everyone else about their terrible behavior.

These folks just did not know me. By this time I had already been awarded custody. Therefore, with this legal tool I intended to get whatever sources needed to help my family. I submitted the application, it was accepted, and testing began immediately.

We make small strides in every effort but the realization is you must be prepared for the rocky ride ahead. It took a great deal of time before I realized that with all the assistance in the world, I would still have to deal with educators, and other professionals that did not share my way of doing things. The biggest hurdle I had to face was the boys attitude and behavior. My lesson, and I learned this quickly, you can't make someone do something that they don't want to do. For me creating change was hard, difficult at best.

There is an unfortunate stigma regarding behavior, children's psychiatric disorders, as well as those persons that require medication and children and adolescents who benefit from receiving special education services. I have no understanding therefore I can't explain this negative concept. I've seen it, heard it, witnessed it, from educators to the secretary who schedules the appointment.

My first time experiencing this I couldn't believe the surprising and disturbing lack of concern for preserving a child's self-esteem. Someone should be concerned about how our children feel about themselves, as well as the struggles they contain within themselves. Special Education is a very broad term that describes specially designed instruction that meets the educational needs of students with a disability.

Over 50% of students with a mental health condition ages fourteen and older served by special education drop out of school. This is the highest rate of children that give up of any disability group. There is a great deal of misconceptions about just what special education entails. We as parents or guardians must use our voices to bring about change.

How can an adult call a child "slow" or "Unteachable?" It is my personal feeling that these stigmas have been allowed to continue for several reasons. One the family members have not had to deal with it personally. Two, I believe people are in denial if their lives are not perfect or the way they feel it should be.

I'd like to share how the process for testing the boys went. This was new to me, interestingly enough when you don't know what to expect it can be a daunting experience. After I met with the Special Education Department Chairperson in my school district, I was able to ask questions and every concern I had was explained. Of course, there was a mountain of paperwork to complete. The testing was completed by a team of Special Education Diagnosticians.

The School Psychologist administers the IQ and other psychological tests, while the Learning Specialist administers the test that assesses the level of educational achievement and ability. The Social Worker administered the test of Functional Behavior Test. There were also assessments by the Speech Pathologist as well as testing for Curriculum Based Assessment.

When the results are explained, there is a parent advocate present (who also has a child receiving special education services) in case there was anything I didn't understand. Also included was one of their classroom teachers. The data confirmed the need for special education services as a student with an emotional and behavioral disability. The new label for school and to receive services was Other Health Impairment and Emotional Disturbance.

What I found interesting is that there is a federal law, (IDEA) The Individuals with Disabilities Act which requires public, private, as well as religious schools to create an IEP for every child receiving special education services. This government mandate is very specific what categories must be met to receive these services. Autism, Blindness, Deal/Hearing Impairment, Speech Impairment, Emotional Disturbance, Visual Impairment, Traumatic Brain Injury, Mental Retardation, Multiple Disabilities, Orthopedic Impairment, and Other Health Impairments are just some of the incapacities.

The next step is the IEP and I cannot express the importance of this document. The Special Education Team at the boy's school meets twice a year to review and make any changes if necessary. The reason I note the importance because it is also used in college studies, vocational training, as well as on the elementary and secondary level. I always have this document with me for meetings. The information includes any special devices needed, explains how the disability is treated, and what the caregiver needs to be aware of.

One of my boys receives social security and I bring his award letter to every meeting. The pediatrician, therapist, and anyone working with your child needs to have a copy or be made aware of its contents. I have found it necessary to bring certain information to the attention at various meetings.

It is a common fact that children don't learn at the same speed as others; it is the same with each families' experiences. We are living in a time where it is important to acknowledge food intolerances such as peanut, gluten, and lactose. I have found it necessary to be available for teacher phone calls as well as visiting the school to discuss new or old behavior issues. Any noticeable changes or the teacher may have suggestions to try, I am available.

I realize this is difficult when you must work and you may have a boss that is not amendable to your situation, but I put everything on the line for my children. To me they are what is important. This is something I have had to deal with., and I have found teachers who worked around my availability. We simply do not have enough parents that attend parent conferences or contact their child's teacher to see how their child is doing. A report card does not tell the entire story.

We must always ask questions, consistency is the key. We must empower our children so they will know and believe that whatever path they choose in life, they will and can succeed. Therefore we as parents and guardians instill knowledge and confidence. We must also instill lots of love and most importantly; Be an Advocate.

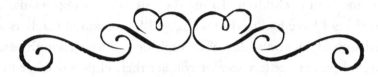

Chapter Four

Living with Children with Disabilities:
ADHD And Related Disorders.

"The first step in the acquisition of wisdom is silence; The second listening;
The third memory; The fourth teaching others." Solomon IBN Gabriol

Before I begin this subject, I must state that my grandchildren have been tested and diagnosed with ADHD Hyperactivity, Oppositional Defiance, and Emotional Disturbance, and Autism Spectrum Disorder. This is an important chapter for me because the information helped me to understand some if not all the behaviors the boys exhibited. I have talked to numerous mental health experts, attended various seminars, talked to numerous parents as we sat for hours in waiting rooms for our children to be seen, and read articles about the massive subject called ADHD. I must confess that the most important things I learned through all of this is I had to LISTEN, rather than speaking.

Also it was important for me to control my emotions, anger, frustration, and fear because you will understand so much more when you are calm. You may not like what the person is telling you but it's important to remove the negative behavior. That enables you to think and develop a plan that will bring positive results.

A valuable tool that several of our therapists used is that children must learn to finish a task, no matter how difficult they think things are, and they must utilize anger management techniques. I thought about how difficult it was for me to control my emotions when trying to get help for my boys, so I began to think how the boys must think when they are faced with challenges. I've seen firsthand how quickly their mood swings would appear, impulsive, or they become easily distracted. In the middle of a conversation, I realize I no longer have their attention. Hyperactivity is not a good thing but it exists in our house.

A problem I have is trying to define the medical problem or diagnosis because there are no reliable blood tests, or x-rays to point out the disorder. Bipolar Disorder is a title that the doctors and therapists discuss in therapy sessions. Along with ADHD there are common symptoms such as energy bursts and restlessness. To add to the mix, some children exhibit bouts of depression.

There are days when I am totally confused as to what symptoms the boys are exhibiting. These disorders are similar in some respects yet they have their own distinct categories. There are so many disorders, labels, and definitions that I have difficulty at times understanding not only what I am reading but hearing as well.

During a session with the school psychologist, I mentioned that while the boys would make up their beds in the morning, when I went to check on them at night the top sheet, blankets, and mattress cover would be thrown in the corner of their room. It was explained in detail the importance of "touch" and "material." She suggested that I stop using a top sheet, the bottom sheet must be soft, and smooth to the touch. Comforter and pillow cases also had to be of a soft material and one pillow was enough.

Something as simple as removing the tags from the back of clothing was a critical issue. No one would believe the arguments about clothing, I had no idea that the feel of their cloths was that important. I've done trial and error with the type of laundry detergent and fabric softer I used. The boys are sensitive to sound yet they seem fascinated with tv and video games being their preference. As I watch them, I am always fascinated.

ADHD and related Mood Disorders speak for themselves. With proper diagnosis and intervention all are highly treatable and manageable conditions. At best, these illnesses remain largely defined by researchers and psychiatrists. Patients and families are sadly struggling to find treatment options. I've experienced too many times that public perception of mental illness is misunderstood and stigmatized.

One evening, I was listening to a radio personality discuss the process he and his wife went through to get help for their son who was diagnosed with Augusber Syndrome. I was excited to hear on a national station the issues that families who don't have this type of platform to make the world aware of the struggles families have in getting the proper care for their children. He repeatedly talked about the fact that they were able to find help for his son while he was still at an early age.

This statement spoke volumes to me. I have experienced first-hand the problem of receiving the proper help needed but can't because you either don't have insurance or not the right time. We don't accept that insurance is a standard statement in my search for assistance. The fact that this information was on a very popular sports show was exciting for me. I have always felt that the world of mental health need to become an important topic in society.

I was convinced that the boys had Asperger Syndrome. Their Doctor stated that many of the disorders have similar symptoms but they have very distinct characteristics. Borderline Personality Disorder (BPD) is one of the most common and the most serious disorder that affects teenagers. In some cases, symptoms displayed are instability and impulsivity in their behavior and relationships are evidenced in teens that have a diagnosis of ADHD in childhood.

Equipped with this information, I began my search for an explanation or cause for the problem. I found numerous symptoms but I will only define the three that affect my grandsons. Psychological, emotional abuse feelings of low self-esteem, anxiety, anger, loneliness, and neglect was the first. Secondly, there is Biological, genetics play a part and Mental Illness is evident in families. The last one is Environmental, this involves poverty, constantly changing schools, as well as substance abuse by parents.

Research shows that 20% of our youth ages thirteen to eighteen experience severe mental disorders each year. While these disorders affect how our children think and act, at times they affect their coping skills. It is important that every family realizes that having a disability does not define who a person or who the children are. The sky is the limit on what their lives will be. The lives they choose to live.

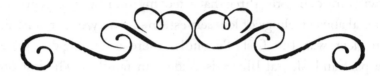

CHAPTER FIVE

Alternative Education vs. Traditional Education

"Everything Seems Impossible Until It's Done."
Nelson Mandela

By the time the boys entered eighth grade, I knew that the traditional mainstream Educational environment was not meeting their needs. Constantly, they were being sent home from school; I had to go to school for conferences regarding behavior. Then there were suspensions from school which meant there was no classroom instructions. That was only a few situations that became a fundamental problem.

While I was in constant communication with the proper educators that were sympathetic, this was something I didn't need or want. What I needed was solutions that I realized that they couldn't give me. It took a supervisor who knew of my families struggles to strongly suggest that I consider a Day Treatment school setting. I did the research because I first needed to find out exactly what were the cons and pros of Day

Treatment versus Traditional Education. Soon I realized that the only choice I had was to go with Day Treatment.

I submitted a petition to the boy's school CSE team (this is the committee on special education) requesting a referral for transfer to a Day Treatment School. After receiving my application, the committee began the testing process. There is always a process and with that, criteria is required for placement consideration.

Information needed: Current evaluation report of disciplinary history and psychological information, Current IEP as well as social history, current treatment plan, and Immunization records. To be accepted into a day treatment setting students must be educationally diagnosed with one or more of the following: Emotional Disturbance, Intellectual Disability, Multiple Disabilities, or Traumatic Brain Injury.

When the testing was completed, I met with the committee to discuss the information they had acquired. One thing I do like is that there is a structure that must be adhered to when a parent meets with the committee on special requests or even if it is just for an IEP review. At these meetings it is mandatory that a general education teacher is present. This is one of the few times I can honestly say that I was happy to be in this meeting.

The general education teacher worked for many years at a day treatment school and he provided questions that I should ask to make sure the school would be able to meet our needs. After the meeting, the committee sent the information to all day treatment schools in our area.

The school I chose, it was simply the place I wanted them to attend, the school reviews all the information submitted to verify that all the requirements were met. Thankfully they accepted the boys and they were to start the next day. All Day Treatment schools are under the authority of the Office of Mental Health.

The school that I fell in love with had the program was designed to meet the mental health needs of children and adolescents between the ages of seven and twenty-one years. These individuals all exhibited problematic behavior. Every one of the behaviors the administrator explained to me were defiance, hostility, negativism, and never accepting their mistakes it was always someone else. There was an extensive list of behaviors that my boys showed.

As she talked my mind was saying check, I knew right then that this would be the perfect learning setting for my boys. To add to my excitement, the school professional treatment team consisted of a consulting Psychiatrist, Psychologist, Social Workers, Clinical Therapists, and a Recreational Counselor. As far as I was concerned, it couldn't get any better. I knew this was an exciting place for the boys the first few days, maybe a week or two, but there would be a time when my happy time would come to an end.

I still felt and feel that day treatment is the best educational setting for my boys who had highly explosive and aggressive behaviors. A special note is the support staff who are trained to handle these behaviors while keeping the boys and those around safe. There are small classes with no more than eight students with a teacher and teacher assistant which complies with their IEP. A school-based day treatment program is consistent with the State Education Department standards for not only the length of the instructional day as well as the requirements for graduation are the same. Students with an IEP can remain in school until the age of twenty-one.

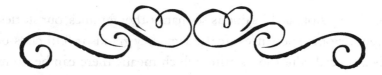

CHAPTER SIX

Understanding The Juvenile Justice System
And It's Effect on The Family

"IT'S BEST TO LEARN WISDOM BY THE
EXPERIENCE OF OTHERS" Latin Proverb

Faced with my grandson's becoming participants of the Juvenile Justice System, I can truly say I never want to experience that day again. I know that there are numerous ways a young person can enter the Juvenile Court System. Accused of a crime, refusal to go to school is a huge problem in my city, running away from home, as well as having a mental health crisis. None of these were issues for us.

Yes, my boys had mental health issues but there was nothing to make me think that either one of them were having a crisis moment. Now my boys were not robbing grocery stores, shoplifting, or bullying other students. Certainly I try to keep a close eye on their free time, I didn't feel that drugs were an issue. To further confuse the matters, going to school wasn't an issue. When they got to school there might be an issue because they were at times disruptive in school.

According to their moods, they would speak in a nasty tone. At times using inappropriate language, they could just be in my opinion—rude. Not just at school, but at home, or anyplace that brought on triggers for this negative behavior. At home they were destructive, there were always instances of finding damage to the walls, furniture, electronics, inside and outside the home. Leaving me as usual unable to determine what started the disaster in the first place.

Sadly, my story is the same as so many other families, our stories are different yet our experiences are the same. My grandson 8:1:1 classroom, this is a special education setting which means there can be no more than eight students, one teacher, and one teacher assistant. We reached the point that if the teacher knew he was going to be absent or would be in meetings and not in the classroom, I would get a call to keep my boy home from school.

Reason for this is because any change in his routine would cause serious complications which usually resulted in his being suspended because of his negative behavior. His teacher was away from the classroom for two days and I received a call that he would be returning to the classroom. Unfortunately, he didn't return nor did I receive a phone call alerting me of this fact.

Well, my boy decided to leave his classroom and roam around the building. He was having so much fun that he decided to run in a different direction from the staff that was trying to save him. Of course this was an impossible task because he felt that it was his right to do as he pleased. The school security didn't agree and tried to subdue my wanderer, only to discover that my eighth-grade scholar, whose grades were excellent, had not only hit this rather large guard but bit him as well.

The school guard insisted on pressing charges. By the time the principal could contact me the police had already arrived. Before I arrived at the school, the police had him in custody preparing to transport him to the adult jail where he would be fingerprinted, booked, and then transported to family court. The officer was kind enough to wait for my arrival and he explained the next set of events that would take place. I felt helpless, couldn't breathe, or think—I was just numb.

After arriving in Family Court, I had to wait for him to be processed. There is nothing to do but wait, people watch, and wait some more. Finally, my grandson's last name was called and we were admitted into the courtroom. During this two hour wait my boy was secluded in another area until it was his time to meet with the judge.

To see him brought into the courtroom in shackles on his feet and hands behind his back in handcuffs was too much for me to take. Waiting for him to be arraigned is nothing like you watch on television. As a parent, I had to face the reality of everything that happened. This was not just my grandson living this nightmare, our family unit would be affected by his actions as well.

The Judge listened to the events described by the prosecution as well as those from his defense attorney. He was detained to a secured youth detention center until his court date. Once a child/adolescent is sent to detention, they can only be released by the court. The court was made aware that he was on medication, so I could take it to the detention facility. I felt a little better when I was informed that a Psychiatrist would handle any medical situations if necessity.

At the next court date, the Judge had been made aware of his ADHD and Mood Order diagnosis, as well as the fact he was receiving counseling. Since this was his first offense coupled with his medical issues, the judge placed him in the JDST program. Juvenile Delinquency Services Team would be working with our family. They consisted of

Juvenile Probation Officers, a Mental Health Counselor, and a variety of specialists.

This process was informative because I gained information about several resources that I felt would help both boys. I chose a program called The Wrap Around Program because it included the family in the development plan as well as it provided intensive community based services. Seventy percent of the youth in the Juvenile Justice Systems have at least one mental health condition and at least thirty percent live with severe mental illness.

There are children and adolescents who live with deep emotional situations as well as mental health issues, things we as adults will never understand. My opinions have changed drastically, I find myself no longer hasty in forming an opinion on certain behaviors because we don't know what my boys and others are dealing with internally.

As we go together through this court experience I've seen what my boy probably thought was just a prank, a way to have fun but, his actions changed into a crime that has severe consequences. I remembered that a Psychiatrist saying the boys have mental issues but some behaviors were choices they make. The medical issues were not always to blame but something within them that they control, the choice was theirs.

There is a statement that I once read and it was brought back to my attention, "KEEP OUR CHILDREN OUT OF THE JUVENILE JUSTICE SYSTEM, IT IS RUINING THEIR LIVES." My response to this, and I know I can speak for every parent, guardian, as well as every adult that sat in that courtroom—please tell us how because I guarantee we will gladly do it.

There are two other components that comprise the Juvenile Justice Department and they are the authority of Family Court; Secured Detention, and Residential Placement. Secured Detention operates 24 hours a day, sometimes it is referred to as a prison for children and adolescents. When you visit you are searched like you are going to prison but it really is for safety measures. I always wished that I could take one of the staff members home with me because not one of these young people gave them any trouble.

When they walk, their hands are behind their back, when they speak or are spoken to all you hear is yes sir and no sir. Residential Placement is court ordered, the Law Guardian develops a plan to ensure that the boys needs will be provided and the state mandates complied with. While the Judge makes all final decisions, she included me in the discussions and plans something she did not have to do. She always encouraged the boys to seek to be the best so that they would be able to make positive changes in their lives.

Both boys lived in a cottage with a housing capacity for only twelve young men, they were all placed by the courts. Residential placement is a twenty-four hour a day program under the clinical supervision of a mental health professional in a community residential setting. Now while I missed them being underfoot at home, I realized that we finally had a situation where they would receive the best care, remain in their school setting so they would still see their friends daily. The amount of change in their lives was at a minimum.

This was important to me, I didn't want them to think that I was throwing away, that I didn't care about them any longer, but I wanted them to embrace the opportunity. The Day Treatment school that the boys attend and the residential placement facility are both a part of a large agency that supplies support to thousands of families. They offer a wide variety of services.

The residential side added to the techniques used to teach appropriate skills on how to change their behavior as well as mental and social adjustments. Doing so, they will be successful at home and in the community. I must admit that it provides a structured living environment with rules and consequences that I was unable to make them follow.

The boys receive intensive counseling, as well as group and individual counseling was needed. They could speak frankly about anger issues and how to manage them. Now, we have participated in these type of sessions before but this was the first time that they couldn't get up and walk away from subjects they didn't want to talk about.

There were home visits but if things didn't go as planned all I had to do was call the cottage and let the staff know to come and pick them up. Staff didn't just pick them up, they had to talk about what happened and what was needed to not entertain those thoughts and actions again. I liked the fact that the placement provided continued treatment in a therapeutic environment. The family unit allowed and encouraged them to play an active role in decisions as well as fun activities. Many days and nights were spent wondering did I do the right thing, then the realization that I had no say in the matter was eye opening. The boy's behavior spoke volumes as to what the next step in their lives would be. I have learned over time that you can't bring change to a person's life if they don't want to change.

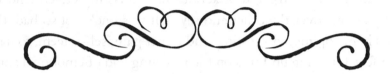

CHAPTER SEVEN

The After Effects of Abuse: Stolen Innocence

"We all survive more than we think we can." Joan Didion

Abuse is a general term that is regulated to someone who causes harm, usually in the form of emotional, physical, or sexual. I have been unable to understand the why, the triggers, or factors which would cause a family member, family friend, or anyone to want to inflict that type of pain. When I became an adoptive parent my world as I knew it became just as complex as my children. My girls exhibited all the signs of abuse.

The Social Worker assigned to my family explained that the child protection workers removed the girls from the mother numerous times and finally the courts removed parental rights which allowed the children to be placed in a safe, and nurturing environment. It was also explained that their mother lacked family support and coping skills necessary to take care of herself, let alone children. There were also issues with alcoholism, drug addition, as well as evidence of mental health issues.

According to the United States Department of Health and Human Services it is estimated that 903,000 children were victims of child abuse or neglect. Upon reading this information, I found it disturbing because of the negative effect of generational abuse in the family. The misconception some people have that physical, emotional, and emotional abuse stops once adulthood is reached.

Sadly, these words, and or actions have a lasting effect. And you can't pick one over the other and say well this one's not so bad, they are all in my opinion disgusting, and inflict pain, self-esteem, to name just a few. Growing up I was on the receiving end of emotional abuse. Neither of my parents chose to be in my life after I was born.

Thankfully, I had a grandmother who took on the parental role and for that I am grateful. Because of her, I didn't have to grow up in foster care or moved from foster home to foster home living with complete strangers. It wasn't until I was well into adulthood that I realized that my parent figure had more issues that she had been inflicted with than I did. I always described my inner feelings and the problems in my life, situations. Aside from being alienated from parental guidance, the most important was the lack of love in my life.

I grew up in an era where parent figures used the extension cord to inflict a 'do right attitude,' or a tool to change behavior. Sadly, these tools just didn't seem to work on me. Did it hurt, yes, but things I wasn't supposed to do just seemed to happen anyway. My parental figure had what I am sure she thought were mind altering "do right fixers."

At bath time, she would wait outside of the bathroom door, as soon as I stepped out of the tub to my surprise the door opens and the beatings began. Another one of her mind changers, which I think was her favorite, she would wait until I was in a deep sleep, then beat me awake. During my youth, this wasn't called child abuse because my friends and classmates, we all shared the same stories.

Yes, I was housed and clothed but there was nothing that I did that was right. The constant negative reminders about my parents or the lack thereof was combined with no family interaction. Negative responses about what my life would be, no instruction about life or what to expect. When I became a parent, I made sure to do the things that I missed out on with my children.

It was important that they knew they were special to me. I exposed them to fun, to enjoy each other as well as how to have goals, and how to interact with other people. I always wanted a family, someone to share everything with, and I know that's why it wasn't difficult to talk me into becoming an adoptive parent.

A young lady came into my life by way of one of my grandsons. Normally, we as parents tend to cringe at the thought of "my baby has a girlfriend." As I looked into her eyes, as well as her body language, I thought this child has experienced a great deal of pain and sorrow. As I learned her story, I was shocked at how she was still standing, how she was even able to function on a daily basis. Her countenance screamed to me that she was a survivor.

The ugly reality of abuse has become a permanent fixture in society. Decades ago, this was a hidden reality of many families, one that was only whispered among certain family members. The result was adults finding out that the person that they thought was their mother was their grandmother, or the person they grew up with as their sister when actually it was their mother. We like to say this type of behavior was in the olden days, not so, it is still a reality today.

An eye-opening experience for me was when my young lady put herself in danger at school. The constant reminders of the physical, as well as emotional abuse from a parent was too much for her and there were times that she tried to take her life. At school, she had taken a large number of pills, as well as inflicting cuts up and down her arms. The school contacted me and as I rushed to the hospital I must admit I was in shock. Yes, I hear of the stories but seeing this tormented act in person was difficult for me to handle.

Too many people in my opinion are living with some type of abuse, but we are afraid of letting go of our past or present situation and breaking the hold. We've allowed our circumstances to control our thoughts, beliefs, and the way we perceive life to be.

There's a young man that shared his story of abuse. His mother would lock him in the basement days on end simply because she told him that she didn't like him and wished that he had died at birth. He cried out for help, but sadly, no one believed him.

The negative effect of childhood memories never goes away, you learn to hide them, lock them tightly in your heart. I've carried inferiority feelings and low-self-esteem around like luggage for years and the word trust means nothing to me. It is non-existent.

I was able to change myself, but it took a while. Honestly, I am still working on it, as well as working with my young lady. One of the therapists for my grandson was working with the boys and myself. Listening to their sessions and attending family support groups, I began to understand that I gave my power away. I really felt that I didn't have a powerful voice. By this I mean I was in control of my actions. I had to learn my worth and this is something I am trying to instill in my young lady.

Is this an easy task, no way; but I had to learn to like myself and realize my worth, and not settle for anything less. I stopped the famous pity parties I had in my mind and I had to allow my faith belief to take over. I made a decision to never let the negative thoughts enter my space, only allowing positive thoughts to enter. For me it is my faith that keeps me going, everyone must find that belief structure that works for them to bring about positive change.

"You can only heal if you forgive, you can only love in peace if you forgive, you can only let go if you forgive. Then and only then, can you truly heal and really love and be loved in return."

Author Unknown

CHAPTER EIGHT

Transition from High School to Adulthood

"A moments insight is sometimes worth a life experience."
Oliver Wendell Holmes, Sr.

As my grandsons reached the golden age of eighteen, they really thought they were grown adults. Little did they know, they were not. If they were grown or "an adult," they would not be calling me daily with "can you take me...How do I do this...I don't have any money...I didn't go to school because I overslept," and the list is endless.

Watching my young men change from the viewing cartoons or playing on the floor with their Legos is bittersweet. As a parent we know the new challenges that they will be facing and questions will always be, "have I prepared them, are they ready to meet these issues head-on."

This is a time that as parents we are nothing more than an ATM, or taxi service. We try to help them recognize their strength to determine what their goals in life are and what they need to do to accomplished them. They also need to determine how they will develop whatever skills they will need in the workforce or college. Finally, how to coordinate all this information for them to use.

This is another battle for my family because of the mental issues and behaviors the boys have exhibited. Now they have decreased, but still there. Plus when you add good old fashion laziness to the mix, this let's me know my young men will still require intensive help to attain self-sufficiency and the freedom they desire. In addition, I am sure there is some degree of fear of the unknown, I feel this is something we all must face at times.

We were at a CSE meeting, I just knew this would be the last one in high school because the boys were scheduled to graduate in the summer. The boys picked the college and program that they wanted to study, I completed their applications, and I thought everything was a go. I began checking prices for luggage, towel sets, and other items they would need to live on their own.

The key to that was, I have-I was-I did, at the meeting I was in for a huge surprise. THEY had not applied the necessary work required to graduate. Therefore they both would need another year before that could happen. One of their teachers said that he felt that the boys found their comfort zone at the school and perhaps they weren't ready to let that go.

I was forced to realize and think about how my grandsons must feel, I had no idea what emotions or thoughts they were experiencing about leaving their school. As I sat there, I had an AHA moment; I immediately realized my problem. I hadn't addressed the obvious, their immaturity and the fact that they weren't ready to move forward. Thankfully both boys have an IEP which will allow them to stay in high school until they turned twenty-one. It doesn't matter if they choose college or vocational training after high school, their IEP will follow with them.

Once I removed ME, I could understand and accept their needs and wants. As parents, we want our children to be successful, there is nothing we won't do for them but with special needs children we can only move back so far. My boys are chronic procrastinators, they will avoid everything until the last minute, and sometimes even past the last minute.

Statistics tell us that students with intellectual disabilities have only a forty percent chance of completing high school. They also have a thirty to forty percent chance of obtaining stable, gainful employment two to three years after high school. I am happy that I started early in their educational process of being a strong advocate.

The CSE committee complied a strong transition plan for each of the boys that would meet the needs of young people with disabilities. Even though my boys were not ready to let their wings soar, they will at least have the tools and skills needed when they leave their high school setting. Real life is a trip without the luggage.

The boys were accepted into a government program called Adult Career and Continuing Education Services. The program works with young people with disabilities and provides services whether they decide to pursue college courses or vocational skills. The boys have mastered several life skills while in high school, but I continued to express to them that being an adult is more than just reaching a certain age.

It was time for them to start thinking for themselves. They also should know how to make the right choices in their lives, especially taking responsibility for their actions as well as the choices they make. A big problem they have is stopping to think before they react—they don't. We in the adult world are forced to deal with various obstacles daily. They will have to learn to adjust their attitudes and make better decisions.

I've given the boys a list of things they need to work on and I have also given myself a homework assignment. First, I should start thinking about what their goals are instead of the goals I would like to see them with. I need to step back, not so far back but enough to help achieve their goals and desires. Let them do the heavy lifting for a change. Most importantly, my remaining role is to be their strongest advocate while allowing them to experience the new challenges that will come their way. Just be there to help them develop their independence.

CHAPTER NINE

Looking into the mirror: A candid look at family survival and mental health

"A Dream doesn't become a reality through magic; it takes sweat, determination, and hard work." Colin Powell

I've met some amazing parents who have shared their heartache and pain, along with the struggles of raising a special needs child. They have shown me by their words and actions, raising special needs children is both a bless and a challenge. While I have never shared with friends just what my small family lives with daily, I found it easy to share with similar families.

This reason being that I've found that people, educators, even some professionals are judgmental about things they have no knowledge about. With these parents, I feel that I can share my fears, as well as all my emotions. With the parents sharing freely their experiences with raising special needs children, I realized that we are all riding the same emotional roller coaster ride. I think it comes down to acquiring knowledge and gaining accessibility to resources.

Now these experiences of meeting and sharing with parents are more common than one would think. Mental Illness is a part of life and special needs parents understand this. Attending a conference for parents and guardians of special needs children, a thought was stressed "when you have an invisible illness you are invisible." I can't wrap my head around the fact that mental health is not treated with the same dignity and understanding that other type of serious illnesses have. What my boys must live with daily, is serious.

I've experienced the negative comments and looks, as well as the incorrect labeling of a serious situation from teachers, and family members. I've even had therapists question my parenting skills, imagine being told that my boys are just "bad boys" who haven't been taught any manners. Saying that they just need discipline. Let's forget about how we as adults feel hearing this and concentrate on how the children must feel when they see the looks, hear the whispers, and hearing these horrid comments.

In my opinion, a major problem for families is the difficulty in obtaining the needed information which would provide help with our children. No one comes into this life with a how-to manual, just think about all the mistakes we would have avoided if we did.

Fortunately, there are some major changes evolving on the national level for health care. Unfortunately, there will not be the same changes and funding sources for Mental Health providers. There is a serious shortage of professional providers who have been trained in the various areas that comprise mental health services for children and adolescents.

Couple this with racial and/or social economic disparity, the business of insurance has created major problems in how services are provided. My family has experienced this with just about every agency we sought help from. Sometimes you wait months to get an appointment. While there are numerous professionals, if you do not have the proper insurance coverage or, like many families, have no insurance then you don't have many choices to choose from if any at all.

To add further stress to an already stressful situation, if you have a government source of payment, your options are slim to none. I don't understand why we are not seeing the masses raising these concerns or our elected politicians screaming for change? In my opinion, for too long the problems of mental illness have been swept under the carpet while it is obvious that there are many who hope these issues would simply disappear. Funding has dwindled severely; hospitals and clinics have closed which impedes the ability for families to receive adequate out-patient services.

A major problem that I see for families like my self is that we keep our children's actions a secret, we don't share what we go through. For instance, it has become the norm that I will have to be direct when trying to get an appointment. You are put on hold for twenty to twenty-five minutes, only to be told I will be right with you, please don't think this is said in a nice office voice.

We as parents must start speaking out. Forget the stigma or comments, "I am sick and tired of being sick and tired." I firmly believe that we need programs that have attainable results, not just saying we have a program and here are the names. I would like to see programs for our youth, adults, and families that are integrated across jurisdictions.

This should include mental health education, provide health services, as well as revamping the entire juvenile justice community. With this our young men and young ladies will have support, education, and they will feel empowered to change their mindset on life. In turn, they will learn their worth and realize that they are important. We must believe that if this information was accessible to everyone instead of the current (what I call) 'so you want information,' then let's play the hide and seek method, find it if you can.

Some issues that I feel strongly about:

1. A need for increased funding for mental health services.

2. We need an increase in the hiring of quailed mental health providers but they need to have training in how to talk to families and patients. They must be concerned for their patients, this is too important to just be a job. My family has experienced professionals meet the children, sit, and develop a plan of action. Then maybe see the child one or if you're lucky two more times. When I talk to other parents you find that this is the norm. How many new people are we going to subject our children; I know I'm tired of meeting them so I can only imagine how the kids feel.

3. A major issue, Insurance Companies need to be accountable for making it impossible to receive care. No money, no insurance, no help.

4. Some professionals, therapists, secretary's, and all that apply— they need to learn people skills.

5. How they should talk to families. We are already living an elevated level of stress daily, so I simply ask is it too much to expect just a little kindness.

These changes and so many more are desperately needed for all the parents, grandparents, brothers, sisters, sons, daughters, and grandchildren. The babies who are suffering from serious mental health illnesses should not feel, see, or hear the negatives, but only the positive. A mental illness does not go away as one gets older, but most importantly, it does not define the person.

It is my desire that by sharing my experiences, it will inspire other families to share their stories. We are our children's strongest advocate and we've been quiet way too long.

"Special Needs Parents are like Superheroes. Wait, Special Needs Parents are Superheroes!! Written by Single mothers who have children with autism. Share If You Agree.

BIBLIOGRAPHY

Children's Mental Health and Mental Health Services

ADHD Justice Support Center. Website: Adhdjustice.add.org/ justice. (2016)

ADHD Therapy-Health Place.com (2016). Child Mind Institute founded 2009.

Alexander, James F, Dr. Developer and founder -Functional Family Therapy for Adolescent Behavior Problems. (2013) American Psychological Association.

Alvarado, Rose PhD, Kumpfer, Karol, Cultural Sensitivity and Adaption in Family Based Prevention. (2015). 2002 – Prevention Science.

Beyond Bars. Keeping young people safe at home and out of youth prisons. The Annie E. Casey foundation. Website: The National Collaboration for youth.

Ceranoglu, T. Attila Dr. Adolescent Psychiatrist. Video Games in Psychotherapy. Published in: Review of General Psychology 2010.

CHADD – The National Resource on ADHD. Provides education, advocacy and support for ADHD. Attention Deficit Hyperactivity Disorder. Website: Chadd.org. (March 2016) Website: CHADD.org.

Child help –founded in 1959 by two parents Sara O'Meara and Yvonne Fedderson. Prevention and treatment of child abuse. National Child Abuse Hotline 1-800-4-A-Child.

Diller, Lawrence, Dr. Behavioral Development Pediatrician. The Last Normal

Child: Essays on the Interaction of Kids, Culture, and Psychiatric Drugs (Westport CT) (2016) Praeger Publishers 2006.

Website: Grand Parents.com. American Grand Parent Association. (Feb. 2015).

Grand Parents Raising Grandchildren. Website: Raising your grandchild.com.

Hurley, Patrick J. ADHD and the Criminal Justice System. Publisher BookSurge. February 22, 2008.

National Center for Mental Health and Juvenile Justice (2015), Website: ncmhjj. Policy Research Associates. Founded 2001.

O'Keefe, Kevin PhD. Horizon Family Solutions. Providing Educational Options for struggling teens since 2001.

Resources for Military families with Disabilities. Center for parent information and resources. March 15, 2017. Website produced by U.S. Department of Education Office of Special Education.

Rosen, Peg, Parenting and Health writer. Questions to ask potential therapists (2016) Website: Understood.Org.

SNRP- Special Needs Resource, Information and Special Needs Resource Project. Resources for parents of children with special needs or disabilities.

Strengthening America Families-funded by OJDDP, office of Juvenile Justice and Delinquency Prevention, (2013), Component of U.S. Department of Justice. Website: ojjdp.gov. Established 1972.

Website: Understanding Special Education, the IPE process and School Success (Nov. 2015).

SAVING THE WHOLE CHILD
READING LIST

Barkley, Russell A. Taking Charge of ADHD: Third Edition (2013) The Guilford Press.

Crone, Deanne, Hawken, Leanne, Horner, Robert. Building Positive Behavior Support Systems

In Schools. Functional Behavior Assessment (2015) The Guilford Press.

Earley, Pete. Crazy: A Fathers Search Through Americas Mental Health Madness (2007) Berkley Publishing

Freiburger, Tina; Jordan, Kareem: Race and Ethnicity in the Juvenile Justice System (2016) Carolina Academic Press.

Frontes, Lison Aronson. Child Abuse Culture: Working with Diverse Families (2008) The Guilford Press.

Jacobs, Thomas A, J.D. What are my rights, Q&A about teens and the law? (2011) Updated Third Edition, Free Spirit Publishing.

Monastra, Vincent, J. PhD. Parenting Children with ADHD. (2014) American Psychological Association (APA) 2nd Edition.

Richey, Mary Ann. Raising Boys with ADHD: Secrets for Parenting Heathy, Happy, Sons. (2012) Prufrock Press. 1st Edition.

Wilmshurst, Linda, Brue, Alan. The Complete Guide to Special Education. (2010), Josey-Bass Publishers, 2nd Edition.

DEFINITIONS

-A-

Academic Intervention Student support services which supplement instruction provided in the general curriculum and are designed to assist students in meeting State learning standards. Must be consistent with the student's Individualized Education Plan (IEP).

ADD/ADHD: Attention deficit disorder and attention deficit hyperactivity disorder are medical conditions characterized by a child's inability to focus, while possessing impulsivity, fidgeting and inattention.

Accommodations: Changes that allow a person with a disability to participate fully in an activity. Examples include extended time, different test format and alterations to a classroom.

Annual Review: An evaluation conducted at least one time per year, for each child with a disability for recommending the continuation, modification or termination of the special education program.

-B-

Behavior Intervention Plan (BIP): Special education term used to describe the written plan used to address problem behavior that includes positive behavioral interventions, strategies and support.

-C-

Community Advisory Committee (CAC): A committee whose membership includes parents of school children, school personnel and representatives of the public. This committee advises the school administration and local school administration and local school boards regarding the plan for special education, assists with parent education and promotes public awareness of individuals with special needs.

Consent: The written approval a parent gives to the Committee on Special to have their child evaluated and receive services. Consent is always voluntary and a parent may revoke it at any time.

APPENDIX

This appendix lists organizations, Internet Sources, and the United States Department of Education, and the Department of Justice Programs.

APPENDIX 1

John M. Grohol, Doctor, Essay written 2011, Mental Health Professionals: United States statistics according to the U.S. Department of Labor, Bureau of Statistics. There are over 552,000 mental health professionals whose focus is the treatment and/or diagnosis of mental health concerns.

APPENDIX 2

NAMI – National Alliance on Mental Illness. (Feb. 2015). Founded by two mothers, Harriet Shetter and Beverly Young. The Alliance works to improve the lives of individuals and families that are affected by mental illness.

APPENDIX 3

Rachel Freeman, PhD, University of Kansas, (May 2015) Website: Specialconnections.KU. Edu. The University of Kansas. Strategies for understanding behaviors that are affected by environment, and certain events, while stressing the importance of Positive Behavior Support.

APPENDIX 4

U.S. Department of Special Education and Rehabilitative Services (2016) Adult Career and Continuing Education Services – Vocational Rehabilitation (ACCES-VR). This program works with the Office of Special Education and community providers to ensure that a youth with disabilities are prepared for employment, post-secondary education and community living. Transition statements need to be included in the IPE by the age of 15. The IEP and 504 plans continue with students until they complete college studies, or vocational training and job placement,

APPENDIX 5

U.S. Department of Health and Human Services

Facts: Young children may show early warning signs of mental health concerns. Research has shown there are often clinically diagnosable evidence which can be a product of Biological, Psychological, and social factors. (2014) This information is Public Domain on the website of Mental Health.gov.

APPENDIX 6

U.S. Department of Justice Programs. (JJDP).

OJJDP Office of Juvenile Justice and Delinquency Prevention was founded 1974. There are training programs, technical assistance as well as strategic planning to meet the needs of youth with behavioral health who are involved with the Juvenile Justice System. Also provided are crisis intervention, and training for youth and families.

ABOUT THE AUTHOR

Ms. GG is the custodial grandmother of twin grandsons. She is devoted to advocacy for children with special needs and has experienced the challenges and negative stigmas families face trying to find needed resources, education, and treatment providers.

Printed in the United States
By Bookmasters